HUNGRY SHARK

OFFICIAL

SHARK-TASTIC

GUIDE

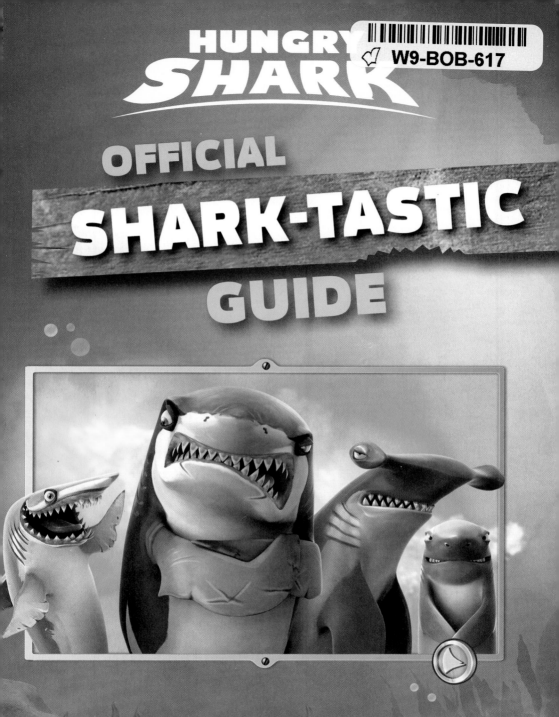

Arie Kaplan

Scholastic Inc.

Special thanks to our chums at Ubisoft and Future Games of London, and a jaw-some thanks to Sam Fry, Valentina Marchetti, Caroline Lamache, Anthony Marcantonio, Lena Barendt, Thomas Veyrat, James Varma, and Giorgia La Rocca.

ISBN: 978-1-338-56873-8

10 9 8 7 6 5 4 3 2 1   19 20 21 22 23

Printed in the U.S.A.   40
First printing 2019

Book design by Carolyn Bull and Becky James

TABLE OF CONTENTS

INTRODUCTION

WELCOME

to the **HUNGRY SHARK SHARK-TASTIC CHARACTER GUIDE**! This is a collection of the biggest chums from the games: heroes, villains, friends, foes, and even some folks who are all of the above! Consider this the **ULTIMATE** menu of shark-tastic info, filling you in on the biggest and best sea creatures in the Hungry Shark ocean!

COMMON SHARKS

These guys are the **BEATING HEART** of the shark crew. And they move to their own beat! They're the core of their coral reef, and whenever something goes wrong in this neighborhood, it's either a problem that these fish caused or a mess they've gotta **CLEAN UP**!

REEF

Reef Shark is the **NEW KID** on the trench. It's easily excited. Don't get it started! This shark is like a kid in a candy store . . . if the candy store was underwater. Its fun, playful attitude means that it makes friends easily, but it also means that people take advantage of it sometimes, and there are days when it finds a **"CHOMP ME"** sign taped to its back.

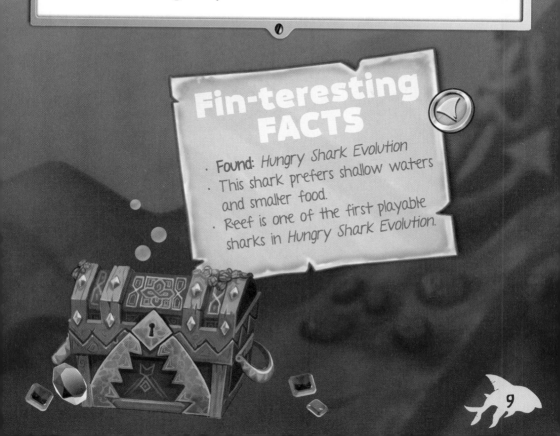

Fin-teresting FACTS

- **Found:** *Hungry Shark Evolution*
- This shark prefers shallow waters and smaller food.
- Reef is one of the first playable sharks in *Hungry Shark Evolution*.

BLACKTIP REEF AND WHITETIP REEF

These two buddies are the same but different! **BLACKTIP** is a little fish with big dreams. Trouble is, sometimes it doesn't realize just how unrealistic its dreams are! Sometimes it tries to plan a great big scheme to catch its next meal without making a plan or following any rules, and everything **FALLS APART**, causing its "next meal" to catch *it*!

WHITETIP lives its life in a constant state of fear and insecurity. It's not just afraid of its own shadow; it's afraid of *everyone else's* shadows too! It needs **CONSTANT REASSURANCE**, but it's a loyal friend.

Fin-teresting FACTS

- **Found:** *Hungry Shark World*
- Whitetip is actually much stronger than Blacktip Shark!
- These are the two smallest sharks in *Hungry Shark World*.

COMMON SHARKS

GOOD SHARK

PORBEAGLE

Porbeagle is like a **WIDE-EYED** puppy dog, except, you know, a shark. It's clumsy and playful and always looking for some new way to have fun. A total innocent, it will sometimes get in **TROUBLE**, but it never does it on purpose. It's just its nature. It's very childlike in that regard. **WHO'S A GOOD SHARK?** Porbeagle is!

Fin-teresting FACTS

- **Found:** *Hungry Shark World*
- Porbeagle is one of the first playable sharks in *Hungry Shark World.*
- This funny guy can often be spotted with his big tongue hanging out!

COMMON SHARKS

BLUE-BLOODED

BLUE

This nimble little shark has a taste for the **FINER** things in life and has traveled the world to discover them— it would much prefer to hunt the finest Atlantic **SQUID** instead of sardines. Blue can sometimes rub the other sharks the wrong way with its **SNOOTY** outlook on life, but at its core it's one of the gang.

Fin-teresting FACTS

- **Found:** Hungry Shark World
- Blue Shark is one of the fastest sharks in Hungry Shark World, but also one of the weakest.

COMMON SHARKS

BASHFUL, BUT BIG-HEARTED

16

CARPET

Carpet doesn't want to be the center of attention. Oh, no no no no no! Not at all! It would rather **SLINK** off into the inky depths of the ocean and let the other sharks grab the **SPOTLIGHT**. But despite its bashfulness and often pessimistic attitude, Carpet has a **HEART** as big as a killer whale, and it's always there for the other sharks when they need help.

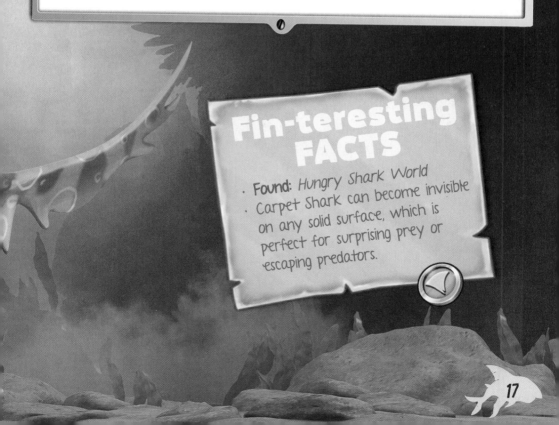

Fin-teresting FACTS

- **Found:** Hungry Shark World
- Carpet Shark can become invisible on any solid surface, which is perfect for surprising prey or escaping predators.

COMMON SHARKS

MAD MEMORIZATION SKILLS

THRESHER

Thresher knows that **KNOWLEDGE IS POWER**. So it works as a go-between for the various shark factions, ferrying information from one group of sharks to the next. The fact that it's able to remember so many facts, figures, statistics, names, dates, and other data makes Thresher feel **VALUED** by the shark community. Because deep down, all Thresher wants is to be loved and appreciated by its peers. What it doesn't know is that they already *do* **LOVE AND APPRECIATE** it! And they're super impressed by this shark's mad memorization skills!

Fin-teresting FACTS

- **Found:** Hungry Shark World
- Thresher is fast and sleek—great at avoiding mines.
- In the real world, thresher sharks are very fast and have an incredibly long tail.

COMMON SHARKS

INNOCENT INVENTOR

HAMMERHEAD

Hammerhead is the chatty mad scientist of the gang. Its head is always teeming with **NEW IDEAS** for gadgets or plans for its latest tech-based project. However, as savvy as it is when it's around its inventions, Hammerhead can be a bit naive when it comes to the outside world. But it has friends to keep it from swimming down the **WRONG PATH**, and it knows how lucky it is to have a wonderful gang of sharks it can truly count on.

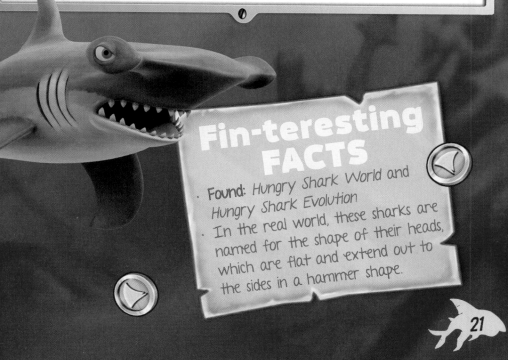

Fin-teresting FACTS

- **Found:** *Hungry Shark World* and *Hungry Shark Evolution*
- In the real world, these sharks are named for the shape of their heads, which are flat and extend out to the sides in a hammer shape.

COMMON SHARKS

GRIN AND
BEAR IT

22

MAKO

Mako's toothy grin frightens many of its fellow fish, but those are just the sharks who haven't gotten to know it. Yes, it does have a big mouth full of **JAGGED, POINTY FANGS**, making it look like a **VAMPIRE**. But Mako is a kind, thoughtful shark who loves its friends very much. It sometimes struggles to express itself and can be a bit weird. But its buddies know that it's a **GOOD PAL**, and that's the *tooth*!

Fin-teresting FACTS

- **Found:** *Hungry Shark World* and *Hungry Shark Evolution*
- Mako is a very fast shark in the games it appears in. Mako sharks found in the real world are also very fast, just like in the games!

COMMON SHARKS

WANNABE HERO

SAND TIGER

Sand is goal-oriented and hardworking. It wants to be known as a **HERO** to its fellow sharks. But its being mean toward others makes the rest of the fish see it as less of a hero and more of a zero. It's one of the **MEANER FISH**, and it needs to start treating its fellow sharks better. Basically, until this tiger changes its **STRIPES**, its friends will continue to see it as just another wannabe.

Fin-teresting FACTS

- **Found:** Hungry Shark World
- Sand Tiger has one of the strongest bites in Hungry Shark World. Its bite is even as strong as larger sharks like Mako and Goblin!

COMMON SHARKS

CLUMSY AND CONGENIAL

26

BULL

Whoa, look out, Bull Shark's coming straight at you . . . aaaand it just **SLAMMED** into a cave wall. Bull may not be the brightest barnacle on the boat, but it has a warm, **WELCOMING** smile and a good heart. It's generally in a good mood, and its **POSITIVE ATTITUDE** is contagious. However, be forewarned: It's pretty clumsy, and if you're not careful, it just might trip over your tail!

Fin-teresting FACTS

- **Found:** *Hungry Shark World*
- Bull Shark is very fast and can eat all the prey in *Hungry Shark World*.
- In real life, bull sharks can live in both salt water and freshwater and can swim far up rivers. Yikes!

NURSE

Nurse Shark is an excellent nurse. However, she also has a **LOUSY BEDSIDE MANNER**. So while she cares very deeply about her patients, it can be hard to realize that since she's often **SNIPING** about how "foolish" those patients are. In short, she has no patience for her patients. The good news is that she'll do what she can to help someone in need. The bad news is that while she's helping you, she's as **SUBTLE** as a hammerhead to the face.

Fin-teresting FACTS

- Found: *Hungry Shark World*
- Nurse has free revive, which allows her to come back to life.
- In the real world, nurse sharks are bottom-dwellers, meaning they swim very close to the ocean floor.

GOBLIN

Like the fairy-tale creature after which it was named, Goblin Shark lurks in the shadows and devises its schemes in private. Goblin is an unusual shark with a strange-looking face, which might be why it **HIDES** in the deep depths of the ocean! When it comes up from the depths, the other sharks have a hard time **RECOGNIZING** it until it's up close!

Fin-teresting FACTS

- Found: Hungry Shark World
- Goblin is a slow shark in Hungry Shark World. It can easily be eaten due to its slow speed.

COMMON SHARKS

ATHLETIC
ALPHA

TIGER

Tiger Shark is the bravest, best-looking, and coolest member of the group . . . er, well, according to Tiger Shark, that is. **OBSESSED** with working out, it wants to win every sports competition it can enter. To Tiger, it's **ALL ABOUT WINNING**, and it never settles for second place. If it *did*, it would probably say that it was the *best* "second place" winner *EVER*!

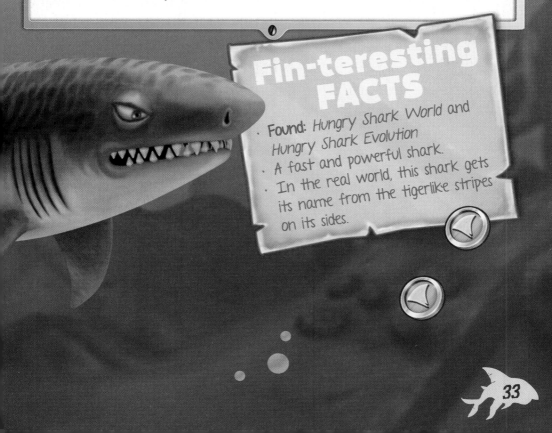

Fin-teresting FACTS

- Found: *Hungry Shark World* and *Hungry Shark Evolution*
- A fast and powerful shark.
- In the real world, this shark gets its name from the tigerlike stripes on its sides.

COMMON SHARKS

MEAN AND MENACING

GREAT HAMMERHEAD

Great Hammerhead, or GH for short, is a maritime mob boss, an OCEANIC OVERLORD. While possessed of great physical strength, GH doesn't want to get its own fins dirty. It would rather have its goons do the dirty work *for* it. You can often see it rubbing its fins together in GLEEFUL ANTICIPATION of some stolen loot its hench-fish have pilfered. Basically, GH can best be described as mean, malevolent, menacing, and about twenty *other* m-words that are synonyms for "evil."

Fin-teresting FACTS

- Found: *Hungry Shark World*
- Great Hammerhead is a very large shark and has one of the biggest health bars in *Hungry Shark World.*

COMMON SHARKS

SILLY SHARK

MEGAMOUTH

Megamouth is the resident jokester and prankster of this undersea gang. If only its **JOKES** and pranks were any good. It's very sociable, but it always tries to sneak jokes into conversations, no matter how **SERIOUS** those conversations are. Mega has one desire: to make everyone laugh. It thinks of itself as the **ALL-PURPOSE COURT JESTER** of the deep. Now it just needs to find an audience that appreciates its unique sense of humor.

Fin-teresting FACTS

- **Found:** *Hungry Shark World*
- In the real world, the megamouth shark is a deepwater shark and is very rare! It only swims in deep, dark waters.

COMMON SHARKS

SLOW AND STEADY

WHALE

Whale Shark is very . . . very . . . very . . . slow. It does things at its own pace and lives life on its OWN TERMS. But this often involves moving as slowly as possible, no matter whether it's eating breakfast or talking with a friend. At the end of the day, Whale Shark is a valued member of the gang and they know that IT HAS THEIR BACKS . . . Even if it is trailing waaaaay *behind* their backs sometimes.

Fin-teresting FACTS

- **Found:** *Hungry Shark World*
- Real-life whale sharks are much less grumpy than this shark. They don't eat much other than plankton and small sea creatures, and pose no threat to humans.

BASKING

Basking Shark is hungry. It's not just in the mood for a little snack. It's **SERIOUSLY HUNGRY** all the time. Basking is constantly refueling. It's a growing fish, and it needs every full meal (including the appetizer and dessert that comes with each meal) or else it gets **CRANKY**. Heck, it's cranky if it doesn't get its after-dinner snack, *after*-after-dinner snack, between-meal snack, post-between-meal snack, pre-snack snack, and midnight snack! It's a full-time *job* **BEING THIS HUNGRY**, and Basking's made it into a career!

Fin-teresting FACTS

- Found: *Hungry Shark World*
- This is a huge shark with an even bigger mouth! It can eat lots of fish at once.
- Size has a downside too—it's easy for this big fish to get stuck in small places.

COMMON SHARKS

BIG-HEARTED HERO

42

GREAT WHITE

Strong, confident, and fun to be around, Great White is the **LEADER OF THE SHARKS**. It has a big heart and would do anything to protect its friends. Great White has an intensely magnetic personality; it doesn't really go swimming around looking for friends, but other sharks tend to seek it out *as* a friend. Just as Great White is never lacking in friends, its friends know that *they're* never alone as long as *it's* around. Great White has always **GOT THEIR BACKS**!

Fin-teresting FACTS

- **Found:** *Hungry Shark World* and *Hungry Shark Evolution*
- Great White appears in every Hungry Shark game! It is always one of the most powerful sharks in the game.

PREHISTORIC
SHARKS

These sharks are **RELICS** from a long time ago! Millions of years ago, they ruled the earth. Now, not so much! But the shark crew has accepted these **OLD-TIMERS** with open fins! Don't call these guys "old." Call them "vintage"!

PREHISTORIC SHARKS

SNOBBY BUT SMART

MEGALODON

Megalodon, or Meg to its friends, is a quiet type. It doesn't talk much, and mostly **KEEPS TO ITSELF**. Some might call it aloof or snobby, and maybe it is. But it's also very smart, and once it's called upon, it leaps into action, **READY AND WILLING** to help out the gang!

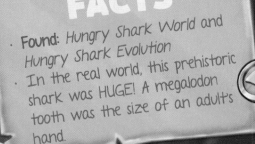

Fin-teresting FACTS

- **Found:** *Hungry Shark World* and *Hungry Shark Evolution*
- In the real world, this prehistoric shark was HUGE! A megalodon tooth was the size of an adult's hand.

PREHISTORIC SHARKS

POWERFUL PROTECTOR AND MATERNAL MANIAC

BIG DADDY AND BIG MOMMA, THE DUNKLEOSTEUS

Big Daddy is a caring guy who looks after his fish with absolute devotion. But that doesn't mean that he's **WEAK OR DELICATE**. If Big Daddy thinks his fish are in danger, he goes from sweet and gentle to powerful protector in no time flat. On the minus side, Big Momma is not the most . . . **FLEXIBLE** shark in the ocean. When she doesn't get her way, she flies into a manic tantrum.

Fin-teresting FACTS

- **Found:** *Hungry Shark Evolution* (Daddy) and *Hungry Shark World* (Momma)
- Big Momma is not slowed down by mine explosions, spears, or other projectiles, thanks to her armor.

PREHISTORIC SHARKS

NAIVE AND NASTY-LOOKING

MR. SNAPPY THE MOSASAURUS

Mr. Snappy might look mean and menacing, but looks can be deceiving. He's actually **VERY FRIENDLY**. In fact, sometimes he's a bit *too* friendly. Mr. Snappy has a tendency to put too much trust in other fish. Because of that, sometimes he gets burned and he ends up **BEING TRICKED**. But if the fish who fooled him ever felt the brunt of his **MIGHTY TAIL SLAP**, they'd think twice about cheating him again!

Fin-teresting FACTS

- **Found:** *Hungry Shark Evolution*
- Snappy can whip prey with his powerful tail and stuns enemies who attack from behind. He also lunges forward with every boost!

LEO THE LIOPLEURODON

Leo is a grumpy old shark, the type who yells at young kids to **GET OFF HIS REEF**. But there's a softie beneath that crusty skin. He can always be counted on for a sarcastic comment, and whenever someone tells him about a plan or a scheme, he's the first to tell them how it could go wrong. But deep in his heart of hearts, **HE'S ROOTING FOR THEM** just the same.

Fin-teresting FACTS

- **Found:** *Hungry Shark Evolution*
- Leo can smash through rocks on the map, using his brute force to carve the world to his liking.

PREHISTORIC SHARKS

SMALL FISH IN A BIG POND

54

SPIKE THE STETHACANTHUS

Spike, or **CHEST SPIKE** if you go by its full name Stethacanthus, is easily startled. That often means a fin full of **POISONOUS** spikes if another shark gets too close! It's a bit unhinged, and people are wary of its spikiness. Little did they know, its spikes and unique **DORSAL FIN** are mostly used for looking cool.

Fin-teresting FACTS

- **Found:** Hungry Shark Evolution
- Spike gets its name from the poisonous spikes on its head. It can stun small fish and fend off attackers using them!

PREHISTORIC SHARKS

CALL ME THE CHAMP!

ECHO THE ICHTHYOSAUR

It's quick, it's determined, and it has to win. Echo is a Jurassic marine reptile who knows exactly where it's going and **WHAT IT'S LOOKING FOR**. With such big eyes and an instinct for survival, it also knows when danger is incoming. Everyone except those **IMPORTANT** to it are beneath it.

Fin-teresting FACTS

- Found: Hungry Shark World
- Echo can spot incoming danger like mines before it even sees them! It can breathe air, so it doesn't take damage on land.

PREHISTORIC SHARKS

NAUTICAL NERD

DRAGO THE PLIOSAUR

Bookish and clumsy Drago is the shark gang's **RESIDENT NERD**. When in social situations with his pals, he usually doesn't know what to say, and he has a hard time feeling like he belongs. But whereas he's the **"ODD SHARK OUT"** underwater, he's also the only one in the gang who can confidently go out on land for any length of time. This doesn't make him feel any better, though. To him, it's just further proof that he doesn't fit in with the other sharks.

Fin-teresting FACTS

- Found: Hungry Shark World
- Drago can bend his neck to gobble up food in all directions.
- He can use his flippers to move quickly on land, where he can breathe air and do no damage to himself.

PREHISTORIC SHARKS

FIERCE AND FRIENDLY

BUZZ THE HELICOPRION

Buzz is fiercely loyal to its friends. Beyond that, it's just plain fierce. So if it's your friend, it'll fight for you **TOOTH AND NAIL**. But mostly tooth, since it doesn't have any nails. Buzz uses its muscles to solve conflicts. It's the **STRONG RIGHT HAND** of the gang. It's not too brainy, and you'll probably never catch it with its nose buried in a book. On the other hand, you'll never find a more generous pal.

Fin-teresting FACTS

- **Found:** *Hungry Shark World*
- Buzz can use its spinning teeth to latch on to helicopters and submarines to cut right through them, and quickly slices up whales, sharks, and colossal squid tentacles.

OTHERWORLDLY SHARKS

Hmmm, how to describe this quartet of **SCIENTIFIC AND SUPERNATURAL** anomalies? These sharks were either home-brewed in a laboratory or summoned by magic! **ROBOTS, AND MUTANTS, AND SORCERERS,** oh my!

OTHERWORLDLY SHARKS

SPACE
SHARK

ALAN: DESTROYER OF WORLDS

Alan is from an **ALIEN WORLD**. He was sent here to destroy Earth. But a funny thing happened on the way to global chaos: **HE STARTED TO LIKE IT HERE!** Alan really appreciates the other sharks, who've become like a family to him. He may be a million light-years from his native planet, but he now considers *Earth* his true home. And he's very **PROTECTIVE** of the friends he's made on this strange new world!

Fin-teresting FACTS

- Found: *Hungry Shark Evolution*
- Alan can use his long, spiked tail to stun enemies and easily gobble them up.

OTHERWORLDLY SHARKS

HE WILL SHOCK YOU

ELECTRO SHARK

Electro Shark is a liar and a schemer, and those are its *good* qualities! A nautical ne'er-do-well who was CAST OUT from proper shark society for its untrustworthy nature, Electro Shark nevertheless found a place within the malicious collection of rogues known as the EVIL TRIO. They appreciate its talent for devious behavior. But do they trust it? To answer *that* question, answer *this* one first: Would *you* trust it?

Fin-teresting FACTS

- **Found:** *Hungry Shark Evolution*
- Electro can stun prey with its Electro Shock ability, paralyzing them to make for an easy snack.

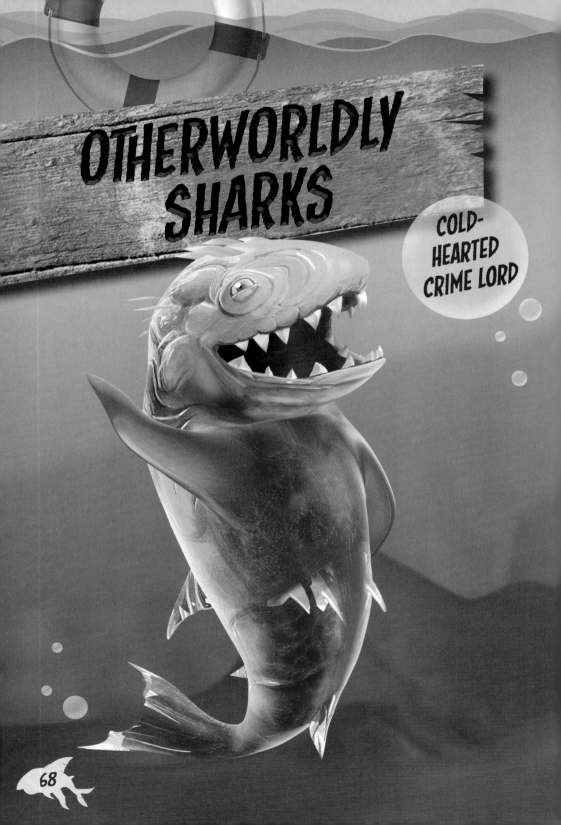

OTHERWORLDLY SHARKS

COLD-HEARTED CRIME LORD

ICE SHARK

A true marine mastermind, Ice Shark is the leader of the Evil Trio. It plots their **CRIMINAL SCHEMES** and takes credit when things go well. But it also denies any responsibility when its plans go awry, always making sure to blame its two friends, Robo Shark and Electro Shark. Its cold heart is only matched by its **SUPER FREEZE BREATH**, allowing it to freeze anything in its path. Cool!

Fin-teresting FACTS

- **Found:** Hungry Shark Evolution
- Ice Shark has Super Freeze Breath—it can freeze things in their tracks and gobble them up!

ROBO SHARK

Meet Robo Shark, the latest in high-tech brilliance. Gasp at its **METAL SKELETON**! Marvel at its infrared eyes, advanced circuitry, and computer brain! It's incredibly innocent and very easy to influence. Also, Robo Shark has a lot of bugs in its system. It will break down at the most **INCONVENIENT** time, and its friends will have to take it in for repairs. If Robo Shark wasn't on the fritz so often, it might've actually developed a personality by now!

Fin-teresting FACTS

- **Found:** *Hungry Shark World* and *Hungry Shark Evolution*
- Robo Shark can eat small mines and fire them as projectiles!

OTHERWORLDLY SHARKS

GIRL ON FIRE

PYRO SHARK

An adventurer with a warm, inviting personality, Pyro Shark is always looking for new experiences to enjoy! She's a **VERY CARING SHARK**, but because she moves around quite a bit, she doesn't have many close friends and can be a bit self-involved. Then again, she's also an **UNDERSEA VOLCANO** who's always oozing hot lava, so perhaps it's best that she doesn't let anyone get too close to her!

Fin-teresting FACTS

- **Found:** Hungry Shark Evolution
- Pyro Shark has the superpower of Dragon Breath—she can breathe flames and set her prey on fire! Did someone say "barbecue"?

OTHERWORLDLY SHARKS

SENSITIVE SOUL

GHOST SHARK

Ghost Shark is a shark of few words. In fact, it doesn't speak at all, but its actions communicate quite a bit. Quiet, contemplative, and loyal, it cares a great deal about its friends. But it does sometimes seem lonely, as though **NOBODY UNDERSTANDS IT**. For this reason, it has trust issues. Maybe it feels alone because nobody else has transparent skin like it does! But its friends try to make it feel like it's the most **BELOVED** shark in the ocean. It's certainly made a splash in their lives!

Fin-teresting FACTS

- **Found:** Hungry Shark Evolution
- Ghost Shark has a "wall pass"—it can pass right through certain parts of the game levels.

OTHERWORLDLY SHARKS

CAMOUFLAGE CRIMINAL

SHARKELEON

The Sharkeleon is a mix between a shark and a chameleon. It's a **MIMIC** who fits in everywhere by copying the personalities of other sharks. It can also blend in with its surroundings. But it's never truly able to be itself. The one thing that defines it is its **UNDERHANDED NATURE**. This, coupled with its talent for camouflage, makes it easy for it to sneak around unnoticed. Because of this, it's turned to a life of crime. So when it's around, just remember to keep an eye on your valuables!

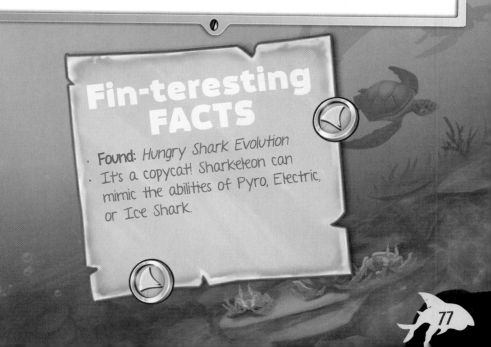

Fin-teresting FACTS

- **Found:** Hungry Shark Evolution
- It's a copycat! Sharkeleon can mimic the abilities of Pyro, Electric, or Ice Shark.

OTHERWORLDLY SHARKS

FEARFUL FISH/
A HOWLING
GOOD TIME

WERESHARK

Behold Wereshark, a combination shark and wolf. When it's in shark form, it's very timid and apologetic. When it's in wolf form, it's **LOUD AND AGGRESSIVE**—a truly big personality. It doesn't have much consideration for those around it, preferring to focus on how much fun it can have and how much trouble it can get into. And the fact that it's the **ONLY SHARK** in the ocean who needs a barber.

Fin-teresting FACTS

- **Found:** Hungry Shark Evolution
- **Moon Rush!** This power lets Wereshark (in wolf form) move much faster than all the other fish!

OTHERWORLDLY SHARKS

POLLUTED PREDATOR

ATOMIC SHARK

The result of nuclear waste contaminating the ocean, Atomic is a mutant that has grown too powerful for its shackles. The glowing green ports that can be seen all along both sides of its body are filled with nuclear **RADIATION**, which powers it like a big battery. On the bright side, it's now one of the few sharks who can walk on **LAND**!

Fin-teresting FACTS

- **Found:** *Hungry Shark World*
- Atomic absorbs toxic waste to heal and charge up, and it can use its legs to move quickly on land.

OTHERWORLDLY SHARKS

CEMETERY CREEPER

ZOMBIE SHARK

Zombie Shark was once a regular Megalodon, but this shark took a stroll in a **CEMETERY** and came back looking like this. Super fast with a **POWERFUL** bite, don't get on its bad side or it might have your brain for a snack!

Fin-teresting FACTS

- Found: *Hungry Shark World*
- Zombie Shark can zombify enemies by biting them!

OTHERWORLDLY SHARKS

OVERSEER OF ILLUSIONS

DARK MAGIC

A learned conjurer of the supernatural arts, Dark Magic is a devotee of every kind of SORCERY found under the sea. Its body is covered in runes, warning symbols, and other glyphs that have some sort of mystic significance. In other words, it's into magic and spell casting, and it's into it *big*-time. So don't ask it a simple question about magic unless you want it to launch into a forty-five-minute rant about the ANCIENT WIZARD MARLIN. (P.S. It's also good at card tricks too.)

Fin-teresting FACTS

- **Found:** Hungry Shark World
- Dark Magic is pretty powerful! It can fire magic projectiles and, with enough charge, a barrage of magic bolts at enemies surrounding it.

FRIENDS AND FRENEMIES

This section is reserved for the **SUPPORTING CAST** of the shark crew. The sharks in this section make up the ever-important group of allies, adversaries, and everyone in between! What makes these **DYNAMITE SHARKS** different is also what makes them unique.

FRIENDS AND FRENEMIES

NATURALLY GIFTED NARWHAL

NATASHA

A true sports whale and a born athlete with a healthy love of competition, Natasha is always training for the next game. She will do **ANYTHING** to win a gold medal . . . anything short of cheating, that is. If dishonesty were a sport, she'd sit that one out. However, sometimes she practices so frequently that her friendships suffer. But Natasha knows that this is an issue and she's working on it! Like Natasha says, **PRACTICE MAKES PERFECT**, whether in relationships or in sports!

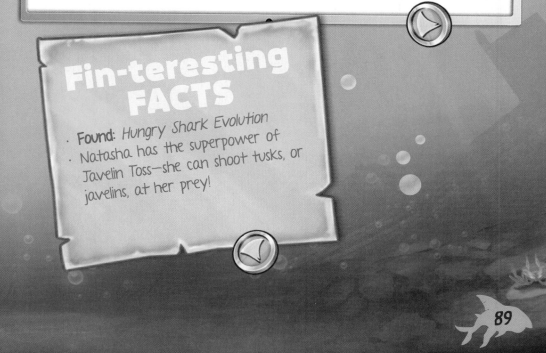

Fin-teresting FACTS

- Found: *Hungry Shark Evolution*
- Natasha has the superpower of Javelin Toss—she can shoot tusks, or javelins, at her prey!

FRIENDS AND FRENEMIES

THE ENEMY OF MY ENEMY

MOBY DICK

Overly cautious and antisocial, with some major trust issues, Moby Dick nevertheless likes the sharks. To him, they're the ENEMIES OF HIS ENEMIES. So they're friends. (As close to friends as *Moby* has, anyway.) Moby sees himself as a noble protector of the seas. It's a job he takes very seriously. Perhaps, it could be argued, he takes his job *too* seriously! Or that he needs to LIGHTEN UP a little. But are you going to tell him that to his face? Didn't think so!

Fin-teresting FACTS

- **Found:** *Hungry Shark Evolution*
- Moby can stun prey by jumping and slamming down onto the water, and firing a burst of water from his blowhole.

FRIENDS AND FRENEMIES

LOCH NESS MONSTER

NESSIE THE PLESIOSAUR

To silence all the doubters, this queen of Scottish lore has emerged from **LOCH NESS** to prove everyone wrong. Nessie the Loch Ness Monster is real . . . and she's *hangry* (hungry/angry)! An ancient protector of the seas, Nessie isn't the friendliest swimmer in the sea. She puts up with other sea dwellers and has a soft spot for sharks. If you're an **ENEMY** of land mammals, you're a **FRIEND OF NESSIE'S**!

Fin-teresting FACTS

- Found: Hungry Shark Evolution
- In the real world, the Loch Ness Monster is a legendary creature said to inhabit a huge lake in northern Scotland, Loch Ness.

94

KILLER WHALE

Despite its scary-sounding name, Killer Whale is the resident peacemaker of this undersea crew! Killer Whale escaped from captivity and is seeking to make the most of **FREEDOM**! Something sharks are experts in. Killer's greatest wish is for all the sea creatures to get along with each other and **HUG IT OUT**! Killer is a whale of a hippie, a total peacenik who just wants to spread its message of love!

Fin-teresting FACTS

- **Found:** Hungry Shark World
- Killer Whale has a bigger jump than most sharks. It performs acrobatic tricks in the air and has an extremely fast boost.
- As a whale, it can breathe air, so it doesn't get hurt if it goes on land!

Hope you enjoyed this **SHARK-TASTIC** guide to the awesome creatures from Hungry Shark! **BE ON THE LOOKOUT FOR MORE** Hungry Shark books in the future!

THE END